Igniting & Inspiring Life-Long Learners

Parents and Educators United as One

By Corri E. Bischer

4-P Publishing
Chattanooga, TN

DEDICATION

To my family for understanding that I drum to my own beat AND still encouraging me to do so.

To my friends for understanding that I drum to my own beat AND you choose to still hang in there with me.

To my children Xavier, Kevin, Shane & Mikayla, I love you all for being my motivation, inspiration and believing in me even when it did not seem to make sense.

The parents and teachers that will read this book and hopefully become inspired and encouraged to continue to do what you do every day and share your gifts and talents with your children and students.

ACKNOWLEDGEMENTS

To my Mom-Thank you about them biscuits and taking baths outside in the pool and all the other fun memories of childhood.

A Special thank you to my Nana, Jamesetta McGee for being the strongest person I know. Thank you for letting me stay right under you and learning so much along the way. Through your life I see what it means to rely on Jesus and let Him be all that I need Him to be and prayerfully, I am all that He asks of me.

Thank you to Dr. Banks for being about your purpose and sharing your downloads with all of us. Thank you for helping me understand that my passion is my purpose and that God has so much more planned for me than I could have imagined.

Thank you to Laura and Wayne Brown and your open dining room table. I have learned so much at The River, where the knowledge and the Kuerig seems to be ever flowing. LOL Mikayla thanks you for the awesome backyard that she gets to spend so much time in.

To all of my friends that I did not mention by name, know that you are in my heart and prayers always. If you are wondering if I am talking about you.....YES, yes I am.

CONTENTS

INTRODUCTION

I am often asked why I choose Howard Gardner's Theory of Multiple Intelligence for the foundation of my teaching. My response is always the same…How could I not?

Gardner asks the question, "How are we smart?" instead of labeling which students are smarter than the others, which ones know how to listen and sit still and then "those" who are always out of their seat. Gardner understands they are all smart and it is up to us to figure out their way of learning and plan experiences that motivate them to learn and be well-rounded individuals. Sounds easy, right? Actually, it is and you will discover why.

We will discuss how to empower parents to know they are the child's first teacher and most influential person in their lives. Yes, parents, you are equipped to provide experiences for your learners regardless of your own educational level.

Teachers, you have a role to play in this day today walk with our children that will have a lifetime effect on them. How many times have you heard a story that started off...”there was this one teacher...” How do you want that story to end when it is about you? Parents and Teachers, we have been given a task that many have slacked on. It is my hope that by the time you finish reading this book and/or go through this training, that you are confident in your ability to teach anyone. I want you to see yourself as not just a teacher or parent, but as a master trainer. The concepts you will learn can also be applied in your own business field or corporate environment. You will learn principles that will work in any environment that you are sharing information with others and you want them to fully understand through active participation.

It is my hope you will see having the ability to train others is a purpose in your life. I also my hope if you realize teaching children is not what you really want to do, you will have the courage to face that and move on to something that really is your calling or purpose. Teachers have too much of an impact on our children for it to be one of negativity and frustration. Even with that being said, write a side note on the side if this is you. Then use the contact me information and I can help you discover your purpose. I also have a colleague that will help you discover how your gifts and talents can turn into income. No excuses why you have to stay if you don't want to.

Be encouraged knowing that we ALL have gifts and talents to give and share. This is what makes us unique and this is what makes our students unique. Get ready for a journey of self-discovery. You will discover how awesome you are and how to bring that same awesomeness out in your children in the classroom or in the home.

Let's talk about Gardner and why I argue he is right on the money with his Theory of Multiple Intelligence. Then, we will discuss how to implement it in our day to day experiences in the home and classroom. But, before we get started, if you would like to take your own personal Multiple Intelligence Test, go to www.Queendom.com, under the IQ test section. This will be informative for you, family and friends.

For ease of reading and spectrum of readers, I will default to trainers and learners.

WHAT IS MULTIPLE INTELLIGENCE?

How are we intelligent? Gardner says we are intelligent in a multitude of ways varying in strength and combination. Gardner defines the Multiple Intelligences (MI) as follows:

Existential Smart- these learners want to know what else is out there. They question if we are here and are we here alone? They have the deep questions to man's existence here on earth. They also question how they fit into the scope of things from a universal standpoint. Why was I created? They will gaze at the stars thinking and believing there is more out there. They often go into religious fields such as pastors, missionaries or life coaches.

Linguistic or Word Smart- These learners use words to get their point across. It may be written word or verbal, as in speeches or lectures. These learners have a lot to say. They are often the ones in class to hold their hand up and respond because they have so much to say.

These are the learners who respond to every Facebook post or comment, just because they have something to say. They are ghost writers, grant writers, poets, bloggers, novelists, authors, storytellers, etc.

Spatial or Visually Smart-These learners see the world as pictures. They see things that many will pass every day. They will recall event and activities by describing what they saw. This could include fine detail that most people would not have paid attention to. This would include things like what people had on or the arrangement of the room. In an academic environment, these learners do best when graphics, photos, charts, and other visual aids are available. They are aware of shapes, patterns and color schemes. You will know a visual learner by the words that they say," I see what you are saying," or "I don't see things that way".

Spatially smart people become your photographers, graphic designers, movie makers, artists such as sculptors, painters, construction workers. When asked, these are the people who will respond to the question "where are the keys?" by telling you to look on the dresser, right next to the cell phone holder on the left hand side. They also drive by recognizing land marks.

Kinesthetic or Body Smart- People who are body smart have a keen sense of what their bodies can do and push it even further. We think of athletes, dancers, actors/actresses, carpenters and construction workers. They must use their gut feeling and react to immediate physical situations. They can be restless and learn best by moving or having the information connected to a movement. These are the children who are also often labeled with attention disorders.

Mathematics/Logical- These are the students who like to work with numbers and logical thinking. They seem to want to always be in the math area calculating or build with manipulatives or blocks. They are students who are systematic in their approach to problem solving and will classify patterns and relationships. They have a logical order of the way things should be done and appreciate routine. These are the people who become engineers, builders, architects, scientist and researchers.

Interpersonal or Self Smart- This type of learner is able to reflect on their own strengths and areas of improvement. They are independent and self-willed. They can be independent minded and may not flow with being in a large group of people. They may like working independently or in close proximity to others but prefers to be left alone. They are considered introverts.

Intrapersonal or People Smart-These kinds of learners are good at reading others. They know how to create a team. They were the kickball captain who would assemble the best players. They can gauge others strengths and see how to use them together for a common goal, personal or in their business field.

These learners are the counselors and mediators. They can help others solve their problems through communication and negotiation. They also have the ability to manipulate situations in their favor depending on the desired outcome.

These are the students who are comfortable taking on a leadership role or are put there by their peers.

Musical or Music Smart-These learners think in rhythm, tone, pitch, intonation, and sound. They are the ones drumming their pencils on the table. Music smart students easily make up songs to remember information. They can easily learn to play an instrument and can often play more than one. They can listen to music and analyze every facet of the piece. Studies show there is a strong correlation with music and math ability. These learners may stay in the music field as composers, song writers, producers or may also go into mathematical fields such as accounting, finance management, etc.

Naturalistic or Nature Smart-These learners would not come in the house if they could get away with it. They are in tune with nature and animals and our connection to the earth as a whole. They believe we are interconnected and it is our responsibility to the earth to preserve it. They see things as it relates to that connection. A flower is not just a flower: it is the origin of an entire life-cycle. Thus, we are connected to that flower. These are the learners who want to dig in dirt, plant things, check out the bugs and what they do. These are the environmentalists and conservationists.

We ARE all intelligent. We all possess these characteristics or learning styles within us. While reading this chapter how many people did you think of friends, within your circle that you could say, "oh yes, this sounds just like so and so?" What would be considered an intelligent person, according to Gardner, would be one who has experiences in each of the intelligences and continues to learn throughout their lifetime.

Therefore, that person is intelligent but also a life-long learner. Most of us would agree that learning is not confined to a few hours per day at school. Their learning is 24/7 because they are curious. Who are you and how do we teach others to become life-long learners?

Notes

USING BOTH SIDES OF THE BRAIN

How do we bridge the gap between both hemispheres of the brain? What is whole brain thinking? What is content and context? How do we ensure that our learners are using all of the bodily functions available to them in order to learn?

The brain is compiled of the left and right hemispheres. There are three modes of processing language and three domains of learning. The English version of that is that our brain has two sides that operate differently. There are three ways the same whole brain takes in information and processes it to react to the messages given to it. Lastly, there are three areas in which the brain compartmentalizes information to be processed or to be stored for later recollection.

The right side of the brain is the artistic and creative side. This is the side that the context of information is processed. This is where you get the artistic, visual, spatial, and humorous information. The right side does well when you, the presenter, have real life example or stories that you can tell to present your case.

The right side leaves the small details left up to the left hemisphere. It is the right brain that process information in order to get the big picture or the "gist" of what is going on. It will listen to the story and get an overall idea of what is being said, but it works in conjunction with the left side that fills in the details with its content. It is this side that triggers "gut", instinct or "going by your feelings".

On the other side, the left hemisphere, there is the content. This is the exact information that is given to the brain to process. This would be the logic, sequential, analytical and rational information. This side thrives off data, explicit information, rules, facts and regulations. As a trainer, when you are presenting, you must entertain this side of the brain with handouts, lecture, text or other factual information that can be researched by the analytical audience. Mind you, understanding Gardner's theory is not to try and change one into a particular intelligence, but it is to provide experiences in each of the intelligences.

How does the brain operate if it is operating in a "whole brain" capacity and how do we make sure that we are purposely setting up strategic experiences to make that happen as our learners are developing? My daughter, who is in kindergarten, complained that they write too much in class. I asked her what were they writing about and why was it too much. She went on to explain that they were growing some tomato plants but the just did the charting She said they were already in small pots when they started.

What I had to understand was she did not get to do any of the actual planting of the plant (teacher said that would take too long), but they did get to count how many inches it had grown and wrote that down. Let me ask this…how much more involved and interested in this tomato plant would she have been had she been able to dig the potting soil out of the bag with a scooper, put it in the cup, put the seeds in the cup and water it for the first time? She would have felt what the soil felt like dry and then wet. She could have looked at the plant and seen and realized these small seeds will later grow into an actual tomato. The two hemispheres would have worked together.

For time sake, this teacher elected to do the real work herself so that she could move on to what she thought was important, the graphing. We have to do better in our teacher trainings to let them know the planting of the seeds are just as important as the charting. If it took all day just to allow the learners to properly plant their own seeds, that could have been the daily activity. We cannot shortchange our learners because we want to be on a tightknit schedule created by someone not in the classroom on a day to day basis. We have to allow time for real learning.

What activity can you recall that you did part of it, that should/could have been done by the learners, but you did it for the sake of time or because you were on someone else's schedule?_____

_____

_____

_____

How do you think your learners would have benefitted more from being able to actually do more of the "hands-on" components of an activity instead of only looking at the end result?

_____

_____

_____

_____

When we look at bridging the two hemispheres, there are some simple strategies to remember when facilitating a lesson. Remember, we want the logical side to cross-over with the creative side. How do we do that? Simple.

Give the big overall picture and then fill in the details with content

- Translate data into charts/pictures/graphs
- Tell a story to illustrate a point

- Talk through the steps as they demonstrate a skill

- Apply specific information to a content

- Allow the students to research something relevant and bring to the conversation via You Tube, Google, PBS Learning media or any other educational websites used.

We want our learners to be able to analyze information for what it is, but also to relate it to something they are already familiar with.

I was blessed many years ago by a man named Brian Kittel with a CD that teaches anyone how to remember everything they want to learn using his techniques. He took the copyright off of the cd and has allowed us to make copies for anyone who wishes to learn the techniques. I called that completely insane because I know what is on this cd. If you want a copy of this CD to learn the strategies first for yourself and then for your learners, please look in the back of this book under resources and I will mail you a copy of the CD.

Using Gardner, we want to use as many of the intelligences as we can to convey the information so our learners can retain it and internalize it. Here are some specific ways to incorporate some of the intelligences in the classroom.

One way would be to allow students to simply state how they feel about the assignment (comfortable, uneasy, nervous, etc.) If you are going to allow your learners to share how they feel about anything, it must be established that your room is a safe

What is a safe room? A safe room is a room where things are shared and it those things stay inside of the classroom (unless there is physical or emotional abuse that warrants further assistance). Safe simply means that everyone is valid, and valuable. It is a room that snickering, verbal or physical bullying, or making fun of anyone else is not tolerated in the room. As the facilitator and adult in the room, you are the one who sets the tone for this. Youth, at any age, feel respected and protected if they know someone has their back.

In a safe room, each student needs to have that same protection from the teacher/parent. We cannot pick and choose who we will protect. It is a common assumption that, for example, in a high school setting, that the nerd students would need a teacher to help him/her assert themselves against any kind of bullying. However, it may also be that football jock who needs that kind of protection from his/her teacher/parent if he is teased, even jokingly, about not being as academic as another student. These are stereotypes, but they both have emotions, fears, insecurities and anxiety and in order for you to be "that teacher", you will need to see that.

There may be youth in your class dealing with things at home. When you establish in your classroom or home that this is a place to talk about it, then your classroom becomes a family. Is this possible? Yes, I know that it can be done. Will it be overnight? No, because they already have an idea of you because you are the

18

parent/teacher and your job is to tell them what to do. When you allow them to communicate more of their reality and open up about their lives and feelings, it is then you are into a relationship building process. You establish that it is your classroom or home, but it is also a safe refuge for feelings and relationship building, not for tearing down. For some, this may be the only place they feel like this. However, as a trainer of a higher level, this is one thing that will differentiate you from the rest.

This is why their story about you will be. "There was one teacher who protected all of us…." You cannot do what everyone else is doing and expect different results.

Without needing to be specific on how to implement this, it is still part of MI and intrapersonal and interpersonal intelligence. Why? When you open yourself and allow others to open themselves up to each other, you are creating an opportunity for all involved to explore their feelings. When this is done in a realistic and honest manner, then our youth are not bottled up and waiting to explode. We have seen such a rise in violence in schools because it is no longer the "safe" place to be.

For some students who were going through hard times at home, they could get to school and know that for that block of time, they were safe from hurt, harm or danger. This may have given them the strength to make it through another day and night at home with whatever was going on. That is not the case anymore. Schools have become just as violent as any other place. We have physical and emotional bullying by students and honestly, by some teachers. There is cyber bullying over the internet where one incident can go "viral" or be played 1 million times in a matter of hours or days and will never go away. The violence among girls has constantly increased over the years. School is no longer a safe haven.

How do you make your class a safe haven and give those students at least that one place they can go for refuge? You can by implementing strategies and techniques within your lesson plan that allows each student to voice their opinion, thought, ideas, suggestions, positive criticism, and input about the environment around them.

If it is within the school, learn what the protocol is for making change. If it is something that grieves them about society or an incident that needs to be addressed, discuss social change media like Change.org or other websites dedicated to making a difference.

Gardner's theory interweaves with one another so fluently that it makes it easy to integrate one with another.

We were just talking about interpersonal and intrapersonal development, but we can also include HOW to introduce and develop those intelligences by using the other intelligences. The other intelligences allow the avenues for self-expression and thought. Youth can express themselves through Performance and Visual Arts.

Performance art includes music, dance, and acting among a

host of others. Visual arts include photography, graphic designs, artists, like painters, sculptors, illustrators, etc. This becomes a continuous flow throughout the whole MI Theory.

What can you do in your classroom to be certain your youth have an avenue to voice themselves through one media or another?

_____

_____

_____

_____

How have your students demonstrated their talents or gifts in the classroom? Have you allotted time for the comedian to "do a set"? Do you allow a singer to sing a song for the class? Starting now, do you see the value in allowing these kinds of freedom of expression?

I was listening to a TED TALKS online the other day and I heard one of, I think, the best comments made about teaching. Her name was Rita Pierson, a 20yr veteran teacher. Her parents and grandparents were educators. Unfortunately, she passed away at the age of 61, only a few months after delivered this message in a TED Talks video.

Here is an excerpt from her talk....

"Can we stand to have more relationships? Absolutely. Will you like all your children? Of course not. And you know your toughest kids are never absent. Never. You won't like them all,

21

and the tough ones show up for a reason. It's the connection. It's the relationships. And while you won't like them all, the key is, they can never, ever know it. So teachers become great actors and great actresses, and we come to work when we don't feel like it, and we're listening to policy that doesn't make sense, and we teach anyway. We teach anyway, because that's what we do.

Teaching and learning should bring joy. How powerful would our world be if we had kids who were not afraid to take risks, who were not afraid to think, and who had a champion? Every child deserves a champion, an adult who will never give up on them, who understands the power of connection, and insists that they become the best that they can possibly be."

She concluded with this...

"Is this job tough? You betcha. Oh God, you betcha. But it is not impossible. We can do this. We're educators. We're born to make a difference."   -Rita Pierson

Her video has reached close to 3 million people by the time I was writing this, May 2014. Although she did not create 3 million plus relationships face-to-face, she surely has left a legacy of her own through her students and now the power of the internet. She will surely be missed.

We are talking about using both sides of the brain and the benefits of doing so. What role does physical development play in academic success? Physical development is a key component to not only academic success but confidence as well?

Gardner talks about being body smart. I was at a water fun day at local school. The children had the opportunity to dunk the principal in a bucket of cold water if they could simply throw a softball and hit a round target. It was sad to see a school full of students, continually, one by one, walk away disappointed that they did not get to dunk the principal. Why didn't it happen? I did not see one child who could aim the ball at the target or throw it hard enough to engage the trap. This is a sad state of affairs. Why? Being body smart has a direct correlation with mathematics, science, language, and academics period. Let me explain.

When a person has to throw a ball to another person, several mathematical calculations have to occur.

One, how much projection will they need to get the ball to go the entire distance? Second, at what point do I need to release this ball so that it goes towards the intended target? These were skills that were learned when physical education was kickball, baseball, tetherball, dodge ball, and the dreaded "butts up" (if you don't know what "butts up" is, you have not lived life!). OK, time out for a second- butts up is when you threw a tennis ball against a high concrete wall. If you attempted to catch the ball as it came back to the crowd of players and missed, but touched it, as long as you ran like lightening and touched the wall before someone else threw the ball to the wall, you were safe.

However, if you did not touch the wall before the tennis ball did, you had to go up to the wall with your face towards the wall and each kid got the chance to hit you with the tennis ball. You hated the good players because they would nail you all the time. The other players you could taunt a little because you knew they were not going to hit you. Now, according to today's standards, this seems a little barbaric, but it was fun. OK, times in.

Our students are not playing the kind of games that will help them with their hand eye coordination nor their left-right brain development. Physical Education has time to go sit outside and wait for the bell to ring before the students come back in. This must change.

In fact, there are so many ways we can change this that there is no excuse. One inexpensive (administrators are always harping on cost) way to make sure our students are getting quality physical development is to infuse yoga into the daily routine.

I have heard awesome testimonies about students, especially those with special needs, embracing yoga, not the religion of Yoga. This is simply the movements of physically challenges and mental challenges. These exercises are for muscle strengthening and flexibility for athletes and non-athletes alike. It is a personal development activity so one does not have to get caught up in a competitive environment. We will discuss competition in a few minutes. For those students who are overweight or obese, it helps sheds the pounds while allowing students to work on their own pace. It is also wonderful because it is something that they can carry with them no matter where they are. They can practice at home without the need for any equipment. In fact, in September, there is a National Yoga Day that encourages schools to get the teachers, parents and students involved in yoga. This would be an excellent time to introduce yoga to students as it is the beginning of the year. They are expecting to learn new things already, so we might as well deliver that to them, by way of yoga classes. Again, this is a great opportunity to involve the entire family by holding a yoga class at the school to encourage parents to come out with other siblings.

Another form of physical development that is becoming more and more popular directly in the school is the martial arts (Asian) , which is actually the Montu arts originating 1000's of years before Asia in Kemet. The Montu arts have always been about discipline, individually and as a team. It is no wonder schools that have incorporated the art into the daily lesson plan have seen significant decreases in violent behavior and discipline. It has often been an afterschool or weekend event for those who can afford it.

Now, we are seeing Montu or Martial Arts teachers dedicated to a much broader audience inside of the classroom. Montu or martial arts teaches individual competition and accomplishment as well as it being a team sport. Its primary focus is discipline above all things in order to learn the skills and techniques taught in whichever discipline it may be. There is Judo, Karate, and Taekwondo among many others.

Staying true to our MI Theory, this is also an excellent

way to combine a history lesson on ancient battle techniques with the actual demonstration of such techniques. For students with any attention span issues, the ability to move about in practice and not simply read and write about it would quite possibly hold their attention. However, they can be done effectively so that you are staying true to the MI model or ideal and providing your learners what they need to develop physically and academically.

What physical development are you or your school providing now?

_____

_____

_____

Do you see a direct correlation between the lack of exercise or physical development and obesity in your classrooms/schools? Explain

_____

_____

_____

_____

Do you personally have a physical development or exercise plan that you follow? Why or why not? What are your obstacles?

_____

_____

_____

_____

Do you think your parents and/or learners are having the same obstacles?

_____

_____

_____

_____

What community resources are at your disposal to address this issue?

_____

_____

_____

_____

What can you do, with the administrations help, to overcome those obstacles for both the parents and students? It is most effective when the whole family is on board with   possible change.

_____

_____

_____

Notes

CHARACTER AND PRINCIPLES

How do we instill core values in our learners when we come from so many different homes, backgrounds, religious beliefs and cultural differences? We say we believe that we possess those talents and gifts needed to fulfill our unique purpose on earth. Gardner touches on many aspects of human development, these characteristics and needs are universal to all humans. They are not concentrated to one geographic location, social-economic group, religion or culture.

We all have the need to give love and to feel loved. In the intrapersonal spectrum, we can provide opportunities for our learners to self-reflect on the ways that they feel loved or that they give love. This can cross over into interpersonal intelligence by having a learner come up with a plan how he/she or a group are going to purposely and intentionally show another individual or group love.

One of the word smart learners in the group can write down their intentions and how they are going to carry this plan out. They may want to do a performance, using their musical, performance dance or body smarts to carry it out.

For the environmentally smart, they could easily interject that they will be directing their love to nature. For the existential or spiritual intelligent, they may look at love from a universal point of view that we are only a small part of this web of love. Using Gardner, we are able to quickly provide several experiences that will lead to enhance character development.

Let us continue and look at other characteristics that we would like to see instilled in our children. As I have written them and left a small space for notes, I want you to write down any experience or thought you may have you want to implement once you get back to the classroom. It is often we hear some great information and think that we will remember it because it was so awesome, and then we are not even in the car good, when we are asking, "what did the speaker say about? I was going to remember something about that." Because I know it is not just me, I am leaving space in several places for you to jot down notes, ideas, thoughts, suggestions, etc.

Using Gardner's MI is an effective way to also teach

character development because the two work seamlessly together. We have the capacity to share joy and happiness. What song just does it for you? When you hear this song, you cannot help but to get up and dance.

Find out what that song is for your students and have it playing as they enter the classroom. One that is currently taking the world by storm is Pharell's "Happy" song. I have to admit, I have to dance on that song regardless of where I am or it at least brings a smile to my face. No, I dance.

Your students may be coming from a stressful situation or not, but we all know the power of music. You know when you are in the grocery store and that great music is playing, you are picking up more items because you are singing and remembering when. What would be your "entering the class song(s)"?

_____

_____

_____

_____

Akil Grant, a history teacher says he allows his students to listen to their earphones at a reasonable volume during independent study. He says he sees a significant decrease in distractions in the classroom. So, if music can calm the savage beast, it can certainly work on school-age learners.

We want our learners to have compassion for others. This can only come from being able to see things from another person's perspective. How can you generate opportunities for your learners to get an understanding how someone else's day is?

One teacher arranged for wheelchairs, crutches, eye patches, ear plugs and other items to be brought in and asked that her students give up their healthy able bodies to see what it would be like to be bound by not having mobility or eyesight or significant decrease in their ability to hear. The experiment was life changing for the students for even that short span of one day.

What can you do with your students to show compassion for another group or individual? List some of your ideas here.

_____

_____

_____

_____

How could you follow up with actual people for students to talk to and in some manner help make their day easier?

_____

_____

_____

_____

In my sixth grade classroom, we had 2 bunnies, a guinea pig and some rats. I look back now and think how on earth was I in a classroom and took care of rats. Though it seems crazy now, as a child it was fun. It also taught us responsibility and how to be gentle.

When taking care of animals, you do have to tap into a nurturing caring side, because you know that animal is dependent on you.

Our children may not have the opportunity to take care of a pet at home. One organization, Pets In The Classroom, provides a small grant for teachers to acquire and take care of small animals in the classrooms. Insects or scientific animals like butterflies or worms are not allowed. However, guinea pigs, turtles, and aquariums are allowed.

There are grants are for the purposes of teaching children to bond with and care for their pets responsibly. The welfare of the small animals involved is of paramount importance. In relation to MI, again, we can infuse intrapersonal smarts, nature smarts, and others by expanding the relationship to creative writing, imitating the movements of the animals and so much more.

Music, Physical Education, and classroom animals have been phased out as we knew it. We cannot afford for the things that teach us fundamental principles, core values and enhance our academic abilities to continually be faded out of our learners lives. We all want our children to understand what it is to be humble, happy and responsible. What better way than to provide a relationship with a pet? What can you do to include an animal as part of their classroom environment?

If you cannot have a pet, can you work with a local shelter to allow them to bring animals to school for students to learn to groom them or just take them for a walk?

Write down some ideas or a plan you can see working for your situation.

_____

_____

_____

_____

I also wanted to address the issue of having faith. Let me clarify that I am not speaking of a certain religious faith, but the simple belief in something that is bigger than you. Youth and teens live in a microscopic world that somehow everything revolves around them. This can lead to a self-serving mind-set and even obnoxiousness if not properly addressed. We do want them to understand they are extremely important in this place we call the world, but they also need to understand they are but one component. We will leave religious beliefs up to the parents as we tackle life faith. MI looks at the spiritual world of how we all fit as pieces fit in a puzzle. This is looking at a much bigger spectrum.

What are some activities you have included in your program: 1) to help children realize how important they are to the continuum of the world and 2) for them to discover what role they play in it? If we can get our youth to question and seek answers about these things at an early age, it may help them not make some of the mistakes we made as young adults.

I think the wide spread phrase is," I need to find myself...' Let's help them not have to look for themselves in desperate moments, but start off knowing who they are and how to discover their own personal purpose in all phases of their lives.

Our youth are killing themselves because of cyber-bullying or because a compromising video of them was put on You Tube. They are screaming to us that they do not see anything past their present situation.

They need the faith in themselves to know they can make it through. It is better to have friends and family to support you, but in some situations, it is just you, nobody else. Our learners need to have the faith in themselves to know they have the characteristics that we talked about. They need be confident in that belief system it will work for them. This has to be a life style practice. This kind of spiritual smarts is personal and internal. As teachers and parents, we need to walk in that same kind of faith so that our learners see us and want to emulate that behavior. We have to understand they see more than what we give them credit for. The old saying, "Do as I say, not as I do" simply does not work.

Our learners are observant to situations around them. What works?

- Statements of affirmation are a great way to start the day.

- A declaration-give them a sense of who they are everyday until it soaks in- "I am smart, I am powerful, I am loved." Is a saying the Dr. David L Banks of Empowerment Church in Chattanooga TN has shared with our young learners and several of those working in the field of education have taken it to their school as well.

Early Childhood Center Director, Greta Moon, walks in each room to do the daily declaration. The young learners are ready to say it as soon as she enters the room. We want to say it until they have no choice but to believe it.

- Journal writing-allow them to write whatever they want, however they want to. These journals will not be read by a teacher or parent, but give them time daily to reflect any way that they wish.

What experiences can you create to allow your learners times to really focus on who they are from a spiritual mindset. By learning to tap into intrapersonal skills early in life, it is our hope we can prevent them from having the melt-downs they are experiencing because of guilt, shame and frustration.it is our responsibility, as trainers, as trainers to guide them towards joy, peace, happiness, gratefulness.

_____

_____

_____

_____

THE FAILURE OF TRADITIONAL TEACHING

I chose to use Gardner's theory because it is well rounded and allows both the trainer and learner to be creative. It is creativity that leads to problem solving. Gardner coincides with my personal belief that it is our responsibility to teach our children how to acquire wisdom. We acquire wisdom by learning to ask questions that lead to problem solving.

MI has no choice but to be well-rounded. It is nine different avenues for the teacher to present information to students and for students to receive and display known knowledge. MI allows for trainers to approach a situation from many angles. I think we can agree that no one solution is going to fit every problem.

An effective trainer will create experiences that cause learners to ask questions, to think about the information shared and based on that ask more questions to explore deeper into a subject for answers. What do you do as a trainer to ask pertinent questions to help the learner think about the process?

_____

_____

_____

_____

This is the beauty of MI. When it is implemented properly, a well-rounded approach is imbedded in your everyday environment. It is the trainer's responsibility to present the information to the learners. It is the learner's responsibility to get their own revelation about the information shared. How do we do that?

Dr. David Banks, explains the phases to receiving new information.

1) When we receive information that needs to be processed, our brain matches it up with information that we already have. Our brain asks itself, "have I heard this information before?'

2) If it has heard it before, that information is familiar and our brain can accept that information. However, if this information is new or does not line up with the information that we already know, it is quicker to reject it than to accept it. If it does line up with previous information or can be related to prior knowledge, then it is accepted and continues it process until it is your own revelation.

Since we want our learners to be creative thinkers, we have

to relearn to accept new information shared with us and still continue to ask the questions that lead to problem solving.

Jane Andraka is the mother of Jack Andraka, a 16 year old who has revolutionized the way pancreatic cancer is detected. This is what she said about her son in an interview.

Jane Andraka: "Even when he was small, he was making hypotheses and testing them even though he didn't know he was. He was always testing his environment and seeing what would happen all the time. And so you had to watch him very carefully.

Jack is super curious, so he's always reading, always reading journals and he's online looking up things. He's seeing what's going on."

This is a student who has changed the world of medicine by inventing a more accurate and less expensive way to detect pancreatic cancer. There was a problem, he saw there was a need to fix it, and he used the resources around him to create a new way. Is this not the goal of teachers to instill into our learners? If it isn't, it should be.

When Jack entered a competition for a much larger project, he had to assemble a group of experts to help him with the task. He selected the highest academic achieving teenagers in the world. He was systematic in his approach to this.

Jack Andraka believes that, "The adventure of working with other teenagers is, not to be offensive to adults, but most adults once you're over 30, you have these pre-conceived blinders on, so you can't really do as much innovative thinking as teenagers can."

Can you blame him? Not really. With technology providing you world wide access to information and people, there is no limit. We need more Jacks in the world.

Jack is curious. Jack is resourceful. Jack has intrapersonal skills. Jack is an interpersonal person. Even after a ton of rejections, he kept moving forward. Jack loves to read and understand. He is linguistic and articulate. Jack has mathematical skills and logical thinking skills. Jack is naturalistic. Jack is the intelligent, problem solver we want our learners to become. How do we get them there? I believe by using Gardner's MI.

We can get our learners here by allowing them to explore their natural curiosity. Support them instead of trying to corral them into what we think they should be doing. They will have to be creative to come up with solutions to problems we have never even thought would exist. Creativity spurs the mind to think bigger. Our learners have access to the entire world's information. Why do we stifle them with using such limited-minded information like textbooks that are outdated the day that they are printed?

Here is an example of a lesson plan using MI .Take out a sheet of paper. With the paper horizontal or in landscape, write down the days of the week (including weekends and holidays) in rows down the left hand margin, skipping space in between. Now as columns write the 9 intelligences across the page.

You should now have a grid that looks like this.

MI	SUN	MON	TUES	WED	THUR	FRI	SAT
SPIRIT							
SPATIAL							
MATH							
INTRA							
INTER							
NATURE							
WORD							
MUSIC							
BODY							

I prefer my lessons be based on questions my learners have actually asked about. Think about the last question one of your learners asked you. Now, if this is difficult for you to think of, then that is not a good sign. If we are engaging our learners, they should be asking questions all the time. If they are simply sitting and waiting for class or the day to be over, we are not doing them any good. If that is the case, don't panic,-help is on the way.

On the other hand, you may have learners that are asking questions all day long. You may not be able to get to all of the questions. However, do not let them be ignored. I keep a few index cards and a pen on me at all times. When I hear a question that I know I want to follow up with later, I write it down so I can refer to it later or bring it up during discussion time. This not only gets the question answered, but it validates the learner who asked the question.

They get an understanding that what they asked was important enough to be brought up in the discussion. I believe wording is an important factor. I like to keep it simple by saying something like, "Brandi made a keen observation and asked......" or "Brandon asked something I thought was a key challenge I wanted to present to the class......."

We know that traditional schools with their antiquated methods of teaching, antiquated resources and mentally antiquated teachers are failing our children. There are so many things we can talk about that are not working in the school system. However, we would be here forever and nothing would get solved. We want to look at reasons and solutions.

Our youth learn differently than the past. Our students have on average $600 worth of electronics on them. This can be their phone and laptop alone.

When they are in an instantaneous, right now society, it is extremely hard for us, as educators, to expect them to go back to the way it used to be, because that is where we are stuck. In the past, students relied on the teacher for information. That information was thought to be gold because she/he was the teacher and they knew best and all we need to do is remember that information until the test, fill out the circles and we are good. This is no longer. The game has changed. It is no longer a possession of the information and sharing it out as I wish. Now, we all have access to the information and now the question becomes who knows how to use the resources available to them. We are dealing with an entirely different group of youth. This is still true for a child as small as two.

I was sitting at the front of the bus looking out the window when I heard a familiar cry. It was a cry of a two year old. I turned around to see her reaching for her mother's phone. The mom protested, "No, you can have it later." The crying commenced. As we all do, mom gave in and gave the little girl the phone. She took the phone, swiped her little fingers across the screen this way and then that way and within 15 seconds she was playing an online game. Not just moving the cursor around, actually playing. Have you ever handed the phone to your young son or daughter to program it for you? Do they seem to take so much less time to install the DVD player?

They are wired different because this is all that they know. My son (21yrs) saw a rotary phone and asked me what it was. All I could do was laugh.

As I mentioned earlier, teachers used to hold the information and we relied on that to be true (so many lies!). Now, using MI principles, learners have the capability to find the information through research.

This actually is a benefit for both the teacher and learner. The teacher is not burdened with gathering all of the information and presenting it to students. Learners were usually required to work alone and any collaborative effort was considered cheating. However, in the real world, jobs and business, the focus is building teams to complete tasks.

We had no experience in this team building participating process because we were always taught we were cheating. As educators, we have to fix this.

What experiences do you remember that you think working in a group would have been more beneficial to your learning than you doing the assignment or project alone?

_____

_____

_____

_____

Our schools are holding on to these old methods of teaching. Are you innovative enough to break out of that mold because you know you would be doing your children a better service than the old status quo? What obstacles do you foresee by implementing MI in a school with antiquated ways?

_____

_____

_____

_____

What groups or organizations do you belong to in order to solve problems on a community, state, national or world level?

_____

_____

_____

_____

How can you help your learners discover organizations that are dear to their passion or interests?

_____

_____

_____

_____

Our problems were on our block. We were not too involved in city, state, national, let alone world issues. We had lesson plans that really didn't mean too much because even if we saw them on a map, we had no idea how far that really was. Now, we have the power of the internet. This brings the world into the classroom. There are so many things to integrate in the classroom to teach our children to be world problem solvers. Again, our lesson plans can consist of questions from not only our learners but now through Skype, Google Chat and a host of other methods that we can connect with schools across the nations and countries. Our children can connect with others (interpersonal smarts) and learn about other true cultures and share about our own. With this interaction, we have the ability to stop stereotypes and media propaganda about one another.

This same mindset carries over into the business sector. It is our responsibility to help learners understand how to manage regions, nations or world companies. We have to broaden their mindsets and in many cases that means broadening our own mindsets. Using MI is not only going to stretch the learners minds, but we as trainers and our antiquated ways, must also adapt and stretch our own minds.

We have the opportunity for our learners to practice live applications instead of mock assignments. We have organizations such as Change.org that empower learners in situations that they may feel like they are only one voice.

This is a learning tool (linguistic-writing campaigns) in life skills and causing change (intrapersonal-reflecting on their own values and belief system) when there are injustices or to show support for others (interpersonal smarts). We can use that same opportunity for practical action, can the learners construct something, build something, or invent something that would help a problem? Other MI that would apply could be math/logical, spatial, among others.

What if we integrated our classrooms to model business incubators where the norm is innovation, creativity and collaborative effort? What would you need to change in your room?

_____

_____

_____

How would it be worth it?

_____

_____

_____

_____

By giving our learners real problems to solve, real assessments, real outcomes, they will have the confidence to know they can make a real difference. The way classrooms are set up now with outdated numbers in textbooks and current events that are no longer current.

In my opinion, as I stated earlier, textbooks are a waste of time since we now have options. This may have been protocol back in the day because there really wasn't a way for students to access the things they can now. If learners are working on a project they are passionate about, they will work on it outside of school.

Our learners have the mindset that learning only takes place from 8-3:30pm. They feel like they are free after that point. We want our learners to be life-long learners and understand they will only get a small percentage of their education from school. It is all the other times during the day they will do their real learning. This will be on their own, no test, no assignment, no class, no teacher. MI gives a foundation for this life-long learning because the learner is a participant in choosing what they want to learn about.

Again, this empowerment makes it easier for that learner to

continue to research because they are interested. Another issue we are missing out on is the ability to manage themselves and projects. We have fallen into this notion that management positions mean that you are over someone. You are their boss. When in reality, true management is managing the situation or maintaining the order of things. This does not include people. By maintaining the order of project it means the people are either following protocol to maintain that order or they or not. If they are not, then it is a managerial decision to work with that person or not.

If there is a class project and the person responsible for maintaining the "call list" keeps losing it or does not have a cell phone or notepad in order to keep the information, it is up to the manager to maintain that problem. It is not the manager's duty to "make" this person do right. It is their responsibility to make sure the "call list" is maintained. If this means getting another learner to take over that duty, then the leader is still maintaining the order of things. We must understand we are to teach our young learners how to manage situations, not people. People will come and go, but proper order can be maintained.

If we give our students opportunities in school to properly understand how to manage a project on a small scale and then graduating to a worldwide scale, we can give them something that will last them a lifetime. We must show examples of how to manage one small area and then grow to manage regions, nations or world-wide companies.

Using a team approach with MI, each member of the team

has the opportunity to be valued. Whatever their talent is, it brings something to the table. This can lead to positive self-worth, acceptance, character development, leadership skills and responsibility. When we look at all of the bullying in school and lack of acceptance of other people for whatever reasons, we have tools in hand to address these issues

At our upcoming charter school, Technology Arts & Design Academy (TADA), we have divided the management courses into the four years. The freshman year each student or team will have a self and city project. During sophomore year, each student will have a city wide project such as a fundraiser, event or activity. In their junior year, they will have a nation-wide project such as a Kickstarter campaign, a charity event, etc. Lastly, by senior year they will have a world-wide project to impact another country by stretching their minds to more than what they can see and to dream bigger than what they can see.

What project have you wanted to be part of, but did not get started because of your own personal lack of information and that is what stopped you?

_____

_____

_____

_____

_____

_____

Who can you recruit from your professional team to help you facilitate this kind of learning for your students? Do you need to expand your network of partnerships?

_____

_____

_____

_____

Have you heard any conversations that could develop into any of these level projects?

_____

_____

_____

_____

Now, let us go back to the lesson plan. What question did you come up with? Write that at the top of your page. Now, looking at Monday and your first intelligence, what is an activity, action or experience that you can help the learners create as it pertains directly to the first question above? Continue to complete the grid with that exact question in mind. Your purpose is to provide experiences for the learner in each grid space based on that question.

The beauty of this is that this will lead to further questions. This will be considered your follow-ups. In each of these scenarios, getting to the answer can be a team effort or an individual effort, depending on the teacher and how they operate their classroom. You can mix how the learners find the answer. The fundamental key here is to allow them the creativity and opportunity to explore. If a child is learning about something they are interested in, it is much more likely that they will be engaged and participate.

When you have a well-managed classroom, the learners will be able to create their own lesson plans based on their interests. This again taps into their personal creativity and they will come up with questions that you may not have even thought about. This is when the ability to know your students, allowing them to use their strengths to create teams to work together or allowing those who wish to work alone will come in handy.

This is in perfect alignment with the idea that creativity and the ability to question is the foundation of wisdom. Wisdom is using the information shared with you, the experiences you have and using them to positively affect your decision making process for the future.

In the children's show, Dinosaur Train, Buddy is a curious Tyrannosaurus Rex that questions how everything operates and functions. In every episode he says, "I have a hypothesis!" This is the first step to becoming an intelligent person, to ask questions.

We often hear that we should do what we love and let the money come. We also hear that we should be about our purpose. As adults, we can have very adult oriented purposes that are usually lined up with some social cause or financial goal.

As learners in our classrooms, their purposes are not extremely far from ours, but they certainly are different. As trainers,

I believe we can teach our learners how to approach discovering their purpose at various stages of their lives as they mature. If one has a purpose or a goal that they are working towards, then it gives them a direction or the possibility of a road map. This is true on any personal or academic level. It is also the most personal. This is why I put helping learners understand the process of learning their purpose as the most important thing when it comes to preparing them for life. This is what we as educators claim to be doing. After their purpose, there are a set of core values and principles that we must infuse as part of our daily lives. This is if you are a parent or a teacher, the opportunities are provided every day to establish and instill certain characteristics and principles.

TALENTS, GIFTS, AND PURPOSE

I strongly believe that we all have a mandate or a purpose here on earth. Many adults do not know their purpose. It is said when you know better, you do better. As a Certified Purpose Discovery Specialist through the Institute for Leadership Deployment, it is my goal to help each and every person I meet, to discover their own unique purpose. My purpose is to motivate, encourage and train parents, educators how to ignite and inspire the natural curiosity in our youth. Our youth need to know their true identity and they have a unique purpose to share with this world. Our youth are creative, problem solvers designed to improve this earth. We have to get out of the way and allow them to do that.

When I discovered my purpose, I was liberated. I was free of wondering. Earlier in life, I wondered should I be doing something else or if I was any good at it. I was fortunate because I have been in the field of education for a very long time. I started in the high school Regional Occupational program (ROP). My original reason for taking these classes was because we could leave high school early if you were leaving to go to your ROP job. I chose child care because it made the most sense with my schedule.

Since then, I have always been in the field of education from one aspect or another. It is only until recently did I understand it to be my purpose. I treated it as something that I liked and something that I was good at. When I saw it as my purpose, I began to see the global importance of what I do. I also saw other opportunities allotted to me as a result of knowing my purpose. I saw this as my way of impacting the world by doing what I love to do.

How important is it to help our learners discover their purpose? Their purpose can and probably will change as they mature. However, sharing with them HOW to discover their purpose by asking themselves the right questions is what is important. This goes hand in hand with having intrapersonal smarts, the ability to reflect on oneself and realizing one's own gifts.

Look back and reflect on a time that you knew exactly what you were doing was what you were supposed to be doing?

_____

_____

_____

_____

How engaged were you in the activities and events that went along with that? How can you, after helping your learners discover their purpose, engage their learning, ignite their own curiosity and provide experiences that will be meaningful to them?

_____

_____

_____

_____

How do you help them find their purpose? Dr. David Banks has published a 5 question self-assessment to discover your purpose. If I asked, what would your students say that they were naturally gifted or talented in?

_____

_____

_____

_____

Part of knowing one's purpose, is seeing opportunities of how to create income based on that talent or talents These are advance and mature concepts, but in order for them to take root in good enriched soil, they have to be started while our learners are young. The concepts, vocabulary and definitions must be explained. This may be new information for the learners as well as you, the trainer. What if we as trainers taught our learners these concepts before they went into high school or college? How much time and energy could we save them in college if they knew exactly what major to select and degree needed? We spend a lot of financial aid on changed majors from one thing to another as they "figure out" what they want to do. They would not need to change so often or choose the option of "undecided" because their experience and knowledge will have taught them better than that.

When we look at people like great athletes, we look at the work that they do on the field or court. We rarely get a glimpse of what it took to get to their level. Having a goal of being the best player, owning a multi-million dollar company, or preserving the Rainforest, whatever that goal is, gives us focus and direction.

One long term activity you can do with your students is a backwards calendar. Learners would look at a long term goal of 20 years from now and go back 5 years until they reach to 6 months, a month, a week and each day. Now, they will know exactly what it is going to take for them to reach that long term goal that they have for themselves. Now, along the way, you can use this technique for a shorter goal or project. This will incorporate math/logical smarts, intrapersonal and interpersonal. Our goal is for you to understand that all the things you do, can fit under the umbrella MI. Our goal is to plan experiences on purpose that match the MI theory.

If you are working with Jr High or High School age learners, you may want to do a backwards calendar from the day that they graduate from college. Crossing over into our visual learners, create a vision board that reflects these written goals.

As trainers and learners we are to be deliberate as we use MI theory. We could also include an oral presentation for this project to peers and community leaders. We talked a little bit about broadening our own horizons earlier. This last suggestion stems from the idea that we can have a room full of presentations of learners with grand ideas and goals.

We can use this opportunity to network with a group of people that can provide additional resources and opportunities for our learners to draw from. This could be anything as far as resources for projects, actual internship projects or maybe summer employment. Again, providing opportunities for our learners to use their interpersonal smarts and connect with others normally within their grasp. When others are excited and open to what the learners are doing, it is easier for them to support financially, internships, scholarships etc.

Notes

HAVE CONFIDENCE BUT NEVER STOP GROWING

A single dad walked his five year old daughter to the classroom for her first day of kindergarten as he fought back tears of excitement and anxiety. She was prepared with her new backpack and new lunchbox and walked in like she had been there before. He gave her a kiss and told her to have fun and that he would see her soon. As he prepared to walk out, he looked at her one more time and asked, "Are you sure you are ready?" She looked at him right in the eyes and said, "I was born ready!" He smiled and gave her one more departing hug and walked to the car. He sat in his car at the edge of the parking lot for 30 minutes, tears streaming down his face. He realized the little girl that he knew was maturing and most of all had all the confidence he never wanted her to lose.

Fast forward and few years and that little girl is now a school teacher doing incredible things in the classroom. Is she still confident? Yes, she is. She is confident that she has learned skills, strategies and techniques along the way that have helped her become one of the best in her field.

She continues to grow and develop herself as a person. We often feel like once we have finished school to get that certificate to say we can teach and that is the end of it. Actually, that is just the beginning. It is now that the school education has to either a) kick in and you appreciate all you have learned or b) you find out much of what you learned has to be thrown out and replaced with updated information.

It is my charge to you that you continue your education no matter what level you are on. If you have not received a degree from college, get one. It is certainly not the only route to take after high school, but in the society that we live in, a college degree is a requirement in many areas of employment or establishing oneself as an expert in your field. College is not the only way, but education, knowledge and wisdom to apply those things learned will be crucial in any business or field one may go into. You may think it is not that important or you don't have the time or whatever the excuse may be. Make the time. I told my own sons that it is not just the education you receive in college, but it is the experience and the connections you make while you are there. When you are in college, you are maturing with people who will be your partners, colleagues as you grow in your purpose. It is these people that will help you to leave your indelible mark in the world as you coach them to do the same.

It takes one generation to change a whole family dynamic about higher education. When you can get your child or children to understand the purpose and reason to go and graduate from college, you can set a new norm

Their children will grow up with the expectation that it is expected they will graduate from college. There are too many families that no one went to college. This can be for a variety of reasons. Unfortunately, one major reason is the cost associated with going to college. However, scholarship and financial aid packets are not always properly explained to students prior to going to college. It is easy to not go to college when no one else has gone either.

It is just as easy make a decision that you are not going to be that "only one" that did not go to college. Again, college is for that learning experience and maturing as young adult.

One parent describes her situation as bittersweet. She would get calls from her son who was away at college, on a regular basis. She was glad that he was out and living on campus and all that goes along with that. However, she did begin to notice that at the end of the conversation, she was out of some money somehow someway. He needed a bill paid, rent was due and he was short, he didn't have enough food to last the week, etc.

The calls became less frequent. He started finding his own way to solve his problems. He started spending money more wisely so he wouldn't be short the next month. Although, she loved hearing from him often, she was also thrilled to know he was maturing into a young man. This is part of the process of growing and maturing.

We should always be growing and maturing in our personal life and relationships, but also in our profession. There are countless workshops and seminars to attend throughout the city, county, state and national level. As we have discussed being the example to our learners, this includes our personal growth. We talked about learning how to stretch our minds and in turn expecting the same from our learners. Here is a challenge to you. If you are not a member of an educational organization, find one to join on a local level and a national level. There are too many for me to even begin to start to recommend, but I will advise you to google it and join as soon as possible. Attend local workshops and events so you may come back to your class to let them know what you have recently learned and how you are going to try it out on them.

What this does is gives them the example of how to be a life-long learner. It will leave more of an impression on your learners if you are telling them to go to school and take extra courses or online classes or workshops if you are doing the same. I know that time is limited as a teacher so I know that presents challenges. However, it can be done.

Even with all of the workshops and teachings, always remember to be true to your own style. You will not be able to emulate another teacher because you are not that teacher. Another teacher may have great results because of her teaching style. Just as we have been discussing how the students learn in various ways, the same goes for teachers, parents and educators. Your style is individual for you.

My son, Kevin, was in the 3rd grade when he saw his name on the board to start school with a certain teacher. He was mortified. He asked me could he change teachers because heard how mean and strict she was. He heard rumors of how she kept her kids in from lunch if they did not finish their assignments and she sent learners to the principal's office if they did not turn in their homework. Needless to say, he was quite nervous. At the end of the first day of school, I asked him, "How did his day go." He burst out in laughter and proceeded how she told him and his classmates that she had a reputation to up hold and she needed them to let everyone know how strict she was and that he could go to the principal's office for any given reason. Puzzled, I asked him why he was laughing. He shared that every year she says the same thing to the upcoming learners, but in reality, she was funny, cool and he really loved her class. He said she was no nonsense, but she balanced out having fun in class and getting his work done.

She stayed true to who she is as a person and as a teacher. Her personality was evident in her teaching. She still had a passion for teaching and it showed in her ability to draw her learners in. She used humor in her teaching because she was naturally funny anyway. If you are not comedic person, don't try to be a comedian in the class. It will not go over well.

Bev Bos, Director of a child development center "In a Child's Path" is unfortunately one of a few people that I believe truly gets early childhood education. When you look at her center, you may see chaos. If you look at it from a child's perspective, you see fun and learning opportunities all around them. She believes children should drive their learning and we are there to be a passengers going a long for the ride and asking questions along the way. She is a prime example of an educator doing education as she sees fit and not trying to fit into the box that many have jumped into. She stands true to Gardner's Theory that children need experiences in order to learn. She is quoted as saying, "If it hasn't been in the hands and the body, then it can't be in the brain." She is serious about the hands on approach. I had the great experience of attending a workshop of hers very early in my early childhood education career and it was a breath of fresh air. She validated everything that I knew to do with my students.

However, I worked with several teachers who were antiquated, using dittos and had too many years behind them to keep up with the students. It was refreshing to hear how excited she was to be working with young people and understanding they were going to be messy and loud and adventurous. In a Child's Path reflects exactly that.

At her center, the learners are free to explore. This includes water play, painting, clay, play-doh, and dirt outside. In most centers, these things are reserved for a supervised, timed activity. If you grew up outside like I did, these things are a key component in learning science on so many levels that it should not be limited to a few times here and there. As Bev Bos explains it herself, this is taken directly from her website:

Overall Bev's philosophy is simple and is characterized by these developmental education principles: children learn through play, interaction, problem solving, exploration and discovery. Cooperation is more conducive to learning than competition. Children learn best when they can make choices and set their own goals. Each child is unique. Education is an on-going process, which is enhanced when the child, teacher and family work together.

Just as she is the example of doing things the way you feel they should be for early childhood education, so is, what is dubbed "The Outdoor School" in Chattanooga TN. Its real name is Ivy Academy. This school is dedicated to nature and environmentalists. They are dedicated to an outdoor hands-on approach to learning. They are service oriented and are outside more than they are inside of a classroom. This is another example of a high school charter school staying true to their own identity and allowing those who believe as they do to create a different model of what we have seen as traditional classrooms. They are opening a new campus this year and their enrollment numbers are soaring and have several on their waiting lists. What this tells me is people are embracing a changed classroom. Ivy is responding to that change by beating to their own drum. I applaud them and what they do.

Whose Child is This Anyway?

Our children learn differently, act differently and have a variety of personalities from the time that they are born. As learners and parents, we need to learn some key things about our youth early on. We are universal when it comes to the cry. We know to check for hunger, dryness, boredom or just uncomfortableness their special yelling alerts us to these things and we are able to respond. However, as they grow older and verbal, even though they possibly have the words to say, there are some things that they don't know how to communicate even if they wanted to. For that, we have assessments. This chapter is simply a chapter of references to various tests that will prove helpful when determining what kind of personality your learners are. If you have a class of 20 or your one and only child, these assessments will help you better understand them.

The first one, in my opinion, is the most important. It was created by David L. Banks, Founder of the Institute for Leadership Deployment. It is a Purpose Discovery Test. There are five questions that are designed to allow the user to draw their own conclusion of their given passion and purpose here on earth. It is this passion and purpose that will help drive the individual towards a goal. It is understood that once a person has a goal, they are more focused and driven towards that goal. Obstacles and set-backs may come, but with a purpose or end goal in mind, the obstacles are simply that, something to get through and not something that causes one to stop.

If you are interested in further information about the Purpose Discovery Assessment, please go to my website at www.wakeshfoundation.org or call me at 423 468 9986.

This assessment is for every person on the planet. There are no demographics when it comes to understanding your purpose and your true identity. We live by what we have financially, what job position we currently hold and the title and letters behind our name. However, our goals and aspirations should be about what we were uniquely put here on earth to do. Once we have that revelation, it will drive us and compel us to further that goal and innate desire to fulfill that goal.

Another valuable tool or assessment that I absolutely love is exactly that, learning one's Love Language according to Gary

Chapman, author of the book, The Five Love Languages of Children.

This is an awesome way to discover how your own children or learners receive and give love. Ann Sullivan, a preschool teacher wore an apron every morning with simple stick-ons that resembled an ear, a smile, arms stretched out and a variety of others.

Each morning her students would select which way they wanted to be greeted. If they wanted a hug, they would take the outstretched arms from her apron and hand it to her. She in return, would give them the biggest hug of the morning. She understood that children have their own love language, just as adults do. If you want more information about taking the assessment for yourself or for your learners, the website can be found at http://www.5lovelanguages.com/profile/. You would also be able to take the assessment for adults once you navigate through that page.

The above mentioned are two that I think will be extremely beneficial for you as a teacher and/or parent to understand your learners or children. There are a wide variety of test that will also give you a greater understanding of our youth. Many of them are available online through Facebook and simply doing a search.

As we discussed earlier, use the tools that are available to you to make your classroom exciting and a place that learners want to be in. Some of the tests are so creative that they may ask "What character would you be in Lord of the Rings?" or some other movie, television show etc. You may want your class to do the test at home and come back to discuss their results and if their friends results were accurate and why or why not.

This leads to a discussion on personalities, real people versus made up characters and who decides what the character is going to do and develop in the movie and how do you want to develop yourself.

This is such a great avenue or platform to discuss the interpersonal intelligences that Gardner speaks of. I hope that I am conveying how easy it really is to implement Gardner and the resources available to do so.

As you become knowledgeable in your field or even your niche of teaching, it is important to not only continue to grow but understand that your information is needed for new teachers and to refresh veterans.

We will discuss in the next chapter how to get paid for the knowledge and understanding that you have. It is a matter of growing to be more than just a teacher, but to become an educator that transforms the lives of those around you. There is a special calling to be a teacher. Everyone is not ready, but because you have hung in there until the end of the book, I believe you are called.

SHOW ME THE MONEY!!

This is usually not a phrase that teachers are too familiar with, because of our experience in our respective school districts, lack of public school funding and there would appear to be a nation-wide conspiracy to keep teachers eligible for government aid and living below the poverty level. However, I have wonderful and great news. This opportunity and those like it are available all over the country and yours for the taking.

We are teachers by choice or default. Regardless of how you were ordained into the profession, you are here now. With that being the case, you have some knowledge, experience, triumphs

71

and some defeats that others will pay you to hear about. They may be a first time teacher looking to get some tips on how to manage her classroom, deal with irate parents who really want to believe their child is the smartest child since Einstein, or everything is going awesome and you have that good news to share. Share it and get paid to do so!!

There are organizations, school recreation centers with afterschool programs that you would be able to share your knowledge and experience with them and get paid for it. During the summer is a great time to create teacher trainings for new teachers so they know what to expect. It is also a great time for experienced teachers to get together and discuss what is working and what is not. You will find the teachers that are serious about their profession will pay for courses. Some teachers wait until their district tells them they have to do training, or in service.

We discussed joining educational organizations on a local and national level. It would be my suggestion to start local when seeking venues to speak. One way to do a search is to look for school RFPs. RFP stands for Request for Proposal. This is an organization asking anyone who speaks to send some information, or a proposal, to them so they can determine if you sound like you would be a good candidate or not to speak. Stay encouraged, they have to go through many proposals. As you begin to speak more and more and gain notoriety and experience, you can move into a state and national level. Think about the trainings and workshops you have attended for either work or school that you have last attended.

How was it conducted? Was the information solid and informative? Were you sitting there thinking that you could do a better job?

These are the things you want to think about when you begin to plan what you want to speak about or what they want you to speak about.

Let's make this a little plainer for some people. If you were to speak for a group of 50 educators @ 35.00 a piece, your attendance ticket sales would be $1750.00. Now, let's say you have a training book that accompanies your training that each participant must have for the workshop/training that is another $15.00 per book. Total book sales would be $750.00. Your total for one engagement would be $2500.00. Does this make sense now? Could you use an extra $2500 from one speaking engagement this summer? What if you spoke at 5 conferences for the summer?

As educators we are usually asking our learners to step out of their comfort zone and move to the next level. We have to remember that for ourselves as well. We have to be the example to our learners how we are actually doing what we are asking them to do. Youth today are starting companies at very young ages. They are doing things we wish we could do but did not have the resources. Now, they are able to take advantage of opportunities presented to them. The difference is they recognize an opportunity, seize the moment to take advantage of it and are not afraid to fail. We have to be more like our learners in that way. Do not be afraid to try and fail.

As this book comes to a conclusion, I would just like to

share that I believe each and every one of us has it in us to teach others great things. I think as educators it is our responsibility to share that information. This is why we became teachers. On the next couple of pages, one a reference page to some people mentioned in the book, but also a resource page that has some great websites to use as you look for curriculum, discussion groups amongst teachers, and educational organizations you can either join or look at to be one of their next keynote speakers or break out session teachers. Are you ready to go out and continue to make a difference in the lives of our youth? As my friend's daughter told him with a straight face, a little cute smile and all the confidence in the world, "I was born ready!" and so are you.

Reference Page

"A Promising Test for Pancreatic Cancer ... from a Teenager." *Jack Andraka:*. TED Talks, 01 Feb. 2013. Web. 30 July 2014.

Pierson, Rita. "Every Kid Needs a Champion." *Rita Pierson:*. TED Talks, 15 May 2013. Web. 29 July 2014.

"About." *Howard Gardner*. Blog at WordPress.com. The Bold News Theme., 15 July 2013. Web. 30 July 2014.

Allen, Laura A. "Bev Bos." *In A Child's Path We Care When You Are Not There*. Bev Bos, 9 July 2013. Web. 30 July 2013

Contact Information

I am available for parent, teacher and corporate workshops and trainings.

You may contact me through any of the following ways:

Website

www.wakeshfoundation.org

Email

wakeshfoundation@yahoo.com
Or wakeshfoundation@gmail.com

Phone/office

(423)468 9986 or (423)596 1072

Facebook.com/ourchildcaresolutions

Resources

http://workathomemoms.about.com/od/kidsactivitiesfamilyfun/a/ideas-for-kids.htm

http://www.littledailyplanner.com/activities

www.science**kids**.co.nz/experiments.html

www.chs-wa.org › ... › *Family Support* › *Supporting School Success*

www.sciencebob.com/experiments/

www.todaysparent.com/family/.../20-**fun**-indoor-games/

www.organizingmade**fun**.blogspot.com/p/**kids**-chore-charts-and-schedules.htm

www.leadersoftomorrow**childrenshome**.com

www.sixsistersstuff.com/.../50-outdoor-**summer**-activities-for-**kids**.html

www.fun.familyeducation.com

www.khanacademy.com

Notes and Networking

Write down at least three phone numbers or emails of a colleagues that you did not come here with

ABOUT THE AUTHOR

Corri Bischer is a member of the Kingdom of Heaven. She is a single woman, but has never been a single parent. She is "mom" to four children, Xavier, Kevin, Shane and Mikayla. She has been in the field of education for over 30 years. She has worked in every capacity from infant care to college level tutoring.

She is currently attending Ashford University working towards her MA in Education. Her latest project Technology, Arts & Design Academy (TADA), a charter school to be located in both Alton, IL and Chattanooga, TN.

She currently lives in Chattanooga TN with Mikayla. According to Mikayla, they will be adopting a puppy very soon.

Made in the USA
Columbia, SC
12 May 2020

96636223R00048